EASY PIANO

Disney

A WRINKLE IN TIME

MUSIC FROM THE MOTION PICTURE SOUNDTRACK

9 FLOWER OF THE UNIVERSE

14 I BELIEVE

20 MAGIC

24 LET ME LIVE

30 WARRIOR

36 A WRINKLE IN TIME

29 HOME

40 MRS. WHATSIT, MRS. WHO AND MRS. WHICH

43 TESSERACT

46 SORRY I'M LATE

52 THE UNIVERSE IS WITHIN ALL OF US

Motion Picture Artwork TM and © 2018 Disney

ISBN 978-1-5400-2811-2

HAL•LEONARD®

Visit Hal Leonard Online at
www.halleonard.com

Contact Us:
Hal Leonard
7777 West Bluemound Road
Milwaukee, WI 53213
Email: info@halleonard.com

In Europe contact:
Hal Leonard Europe Limited
Distribution Centre, Newmarket Road
Bury St Edmunds, Suffolk, IP33 3YB
Email: info@halleonardeurope.com

In Australia contact:
Hal Leonard Australia Pty. Ltd.
4 Lentara Court
Cheltenham, Victoria, 3192 Australia
Email: info@halleonard.com.au

FLOWER OF THE UNIVERSE

Music and Lyrics by SADE ADU,
BEN TRAVERS and ANDREW HALE

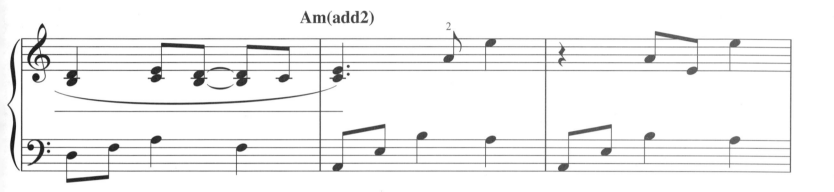

10

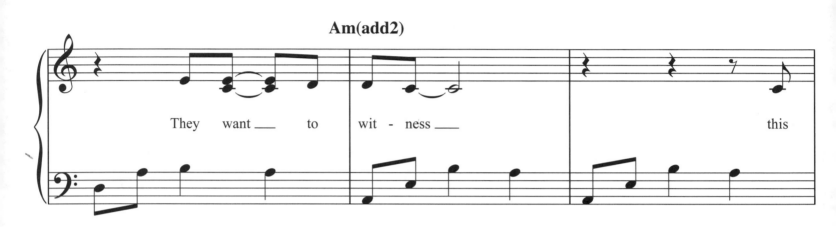

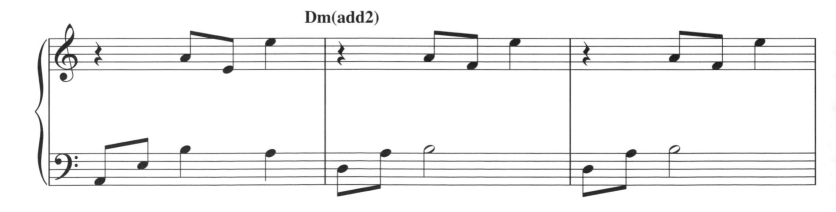

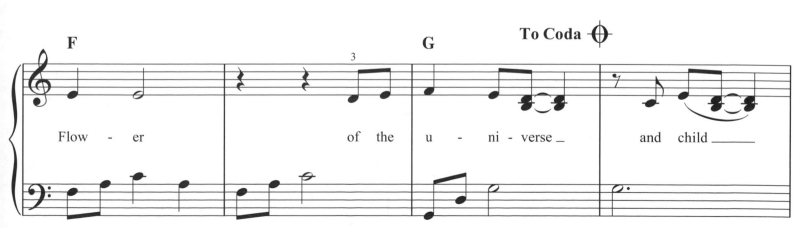

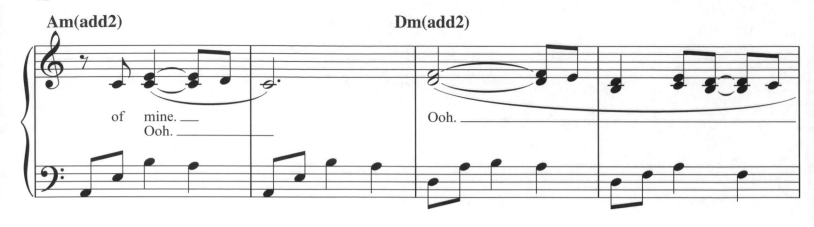

of mine. ___
Ooh. ___

Ooh. ___

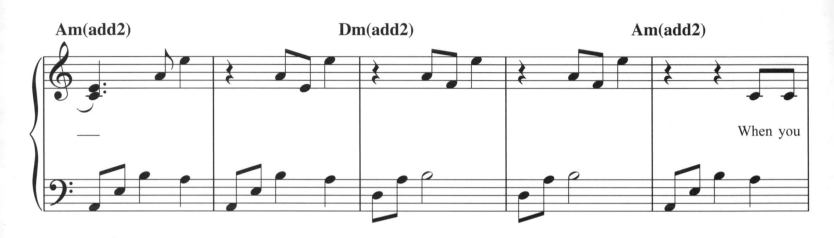

___

When you

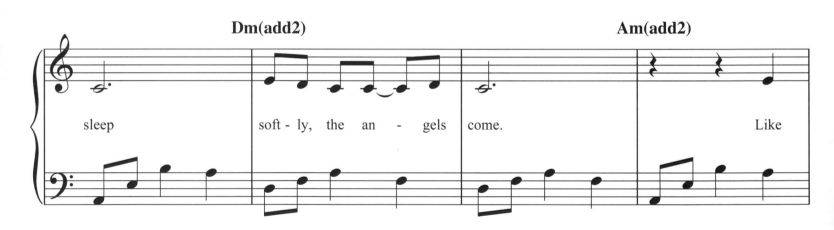

sleep   soft - ly, the an - gels come.

Like

dia - monds,   like my love. ___

They want ___ to

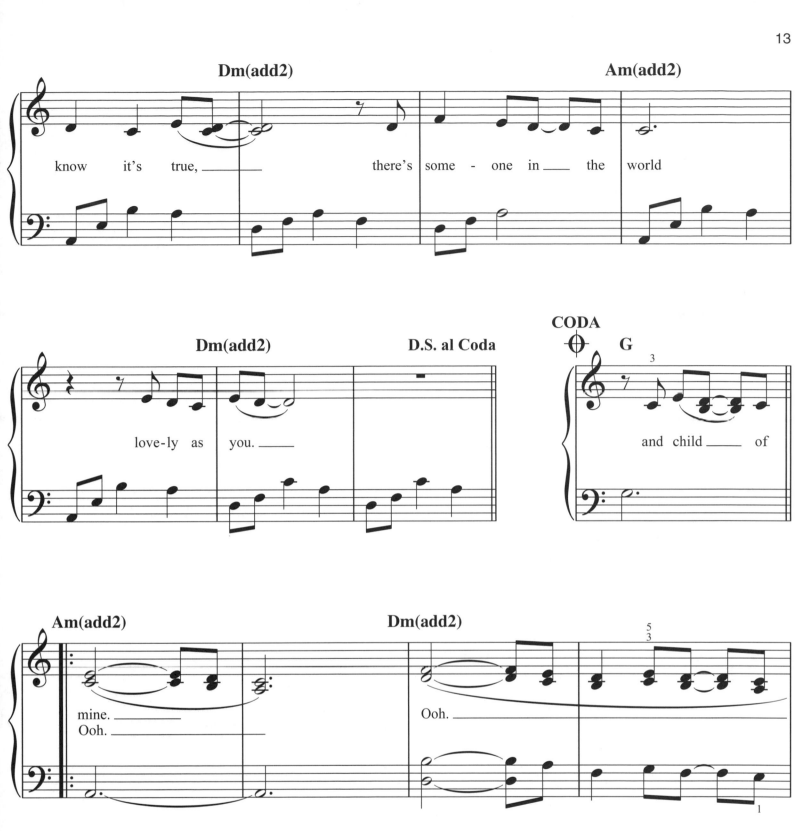

Dm(add2)   **Am(add2)**

know   it's   true, _____ there's some - one in ___ the world

Dm(add2)   **D.S. al Coda**   **CODA**   **G**

love-ly   as   you. _____   and   child ___ of

Am(add2)   **Dm(add2)**

mine. _____
Ooh. _____   Ooh. _____

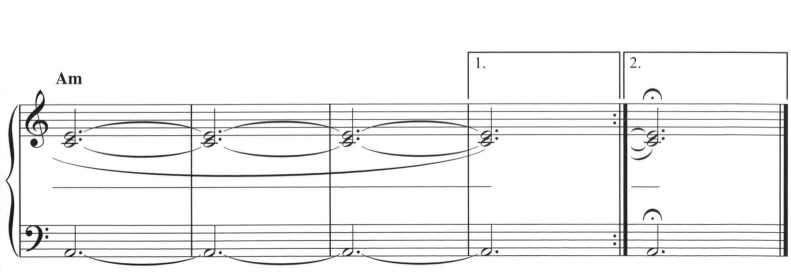

Am

1.

2.

I BELIEVE

Words and Music by KHALED KHALED,
DEMI LOVATO, DENISIA ANDREWS
and BRITTANY CONEY

Moderate Pop Ballad

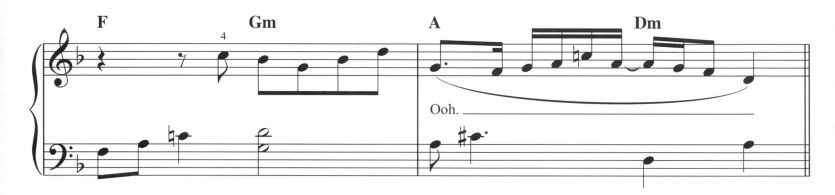

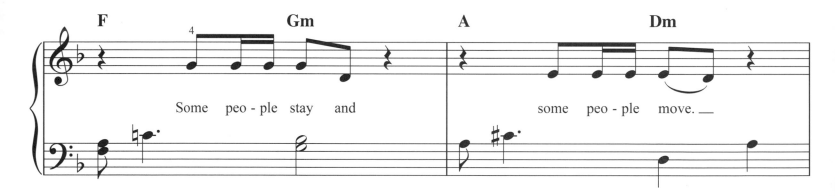

As long as you've got hope, you'll find your way. ___

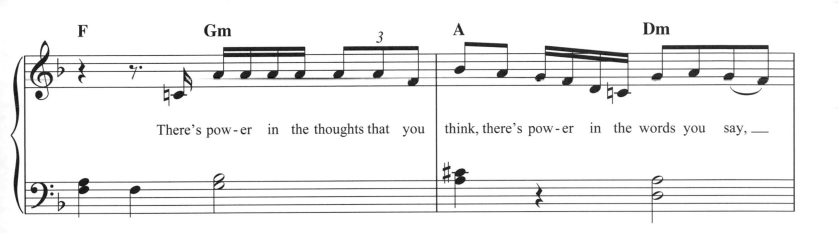

There's pow-er in the thoughts that you think, there's pow-er in the words you say, ___

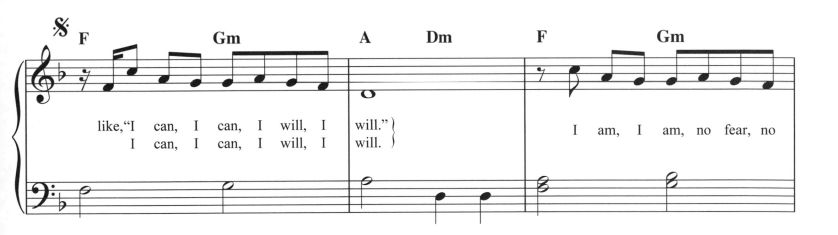

like, "I can, I can, I will, I will."
I can, I can, I will, I will.

I am, I am, no fear, no

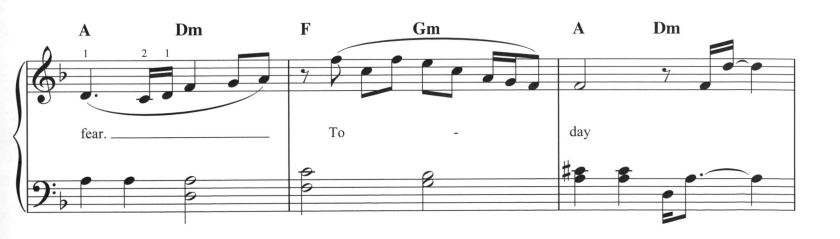

fear. _____ To - day

I saw a rain-bow in — the rain. It told me I can do —

an - y - thing — if I be-lieve, I be-lieve, I be-lieve in me. I be-

To Coda

lieve, I be - lieve, I be - lieve in me.

Ooh, _____ yeah. —

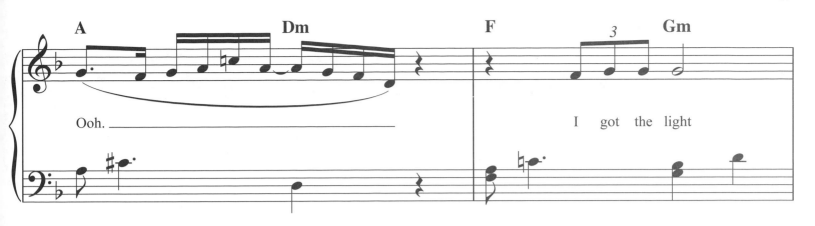

Ooh. _____

I got the light

in-side of me, __ and I've got no choice but to let it breathe. _____

As long as there is love, __ I can make it an-y-where I go. __

If I fol-low my dreams, I'll end up build-ing a yel-low brick road. __

D.S. al Coda

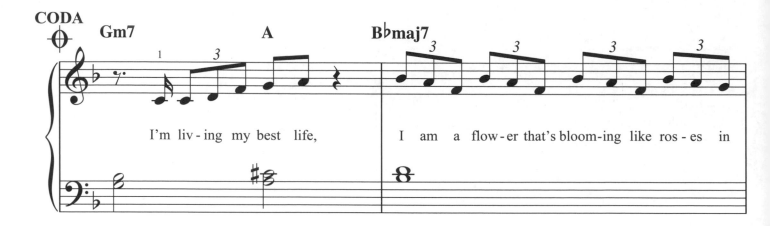

CODA

I'm liv-ing my best life, I am a flow-er that's bloom-ing like ros-es in

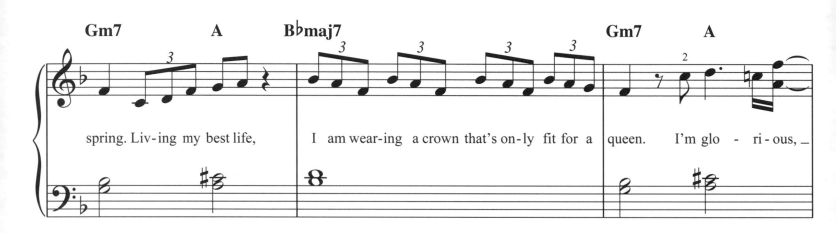

spring. Liv-ing my best life, I am wear-ing a crown that's on-ly fit for a queen. I'm glo - ri - ous, __

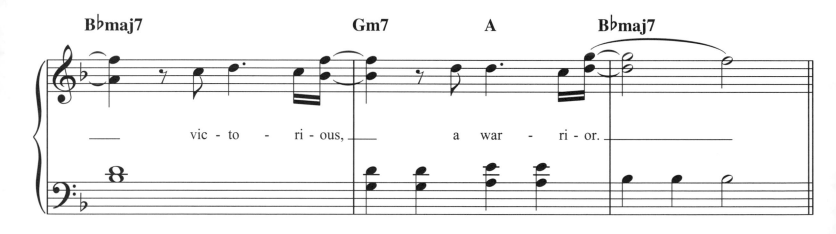

__ vic - to - ri - ous, __ a war - ri - or. __

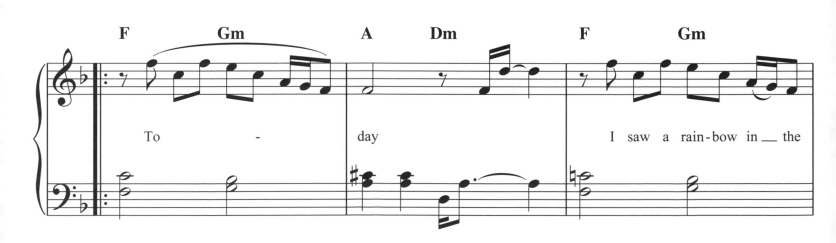

To - day I saw a rain-bow in __ the

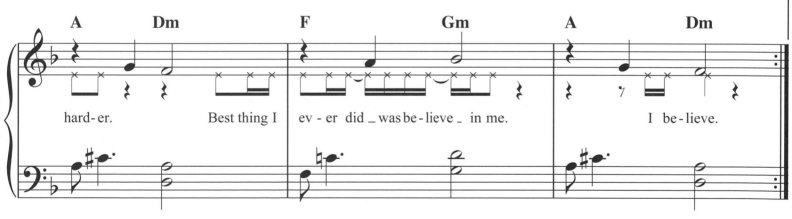

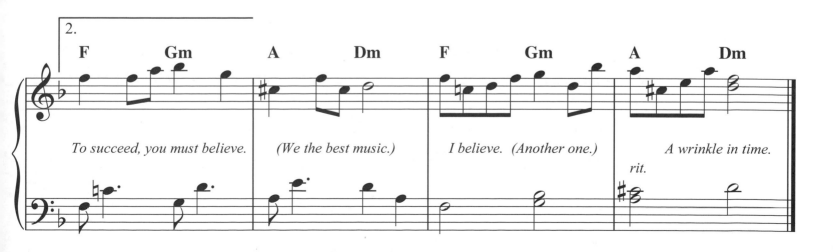

MAGIC

Words and Music by SIA FURLER
and JESSE SHATKIN

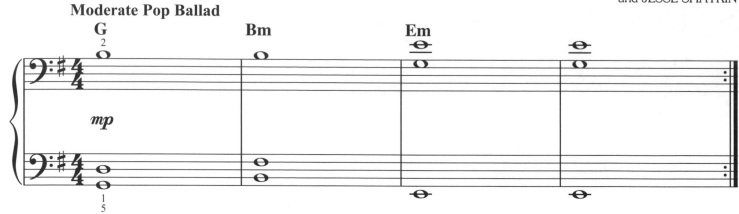

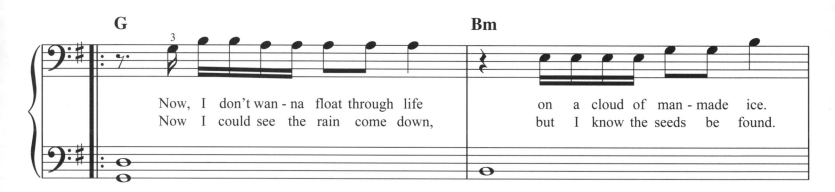

Now, I don't wan-na float through life
Now I could see the rain come down,

on a cloud of man-made ice.
but I know the seeds be found.

Don't want it to pass me by,
I'm gon' watch 'em grow up now,

don't want it to pass me by. ___
I'm gon' watch 'em grow up now. ___

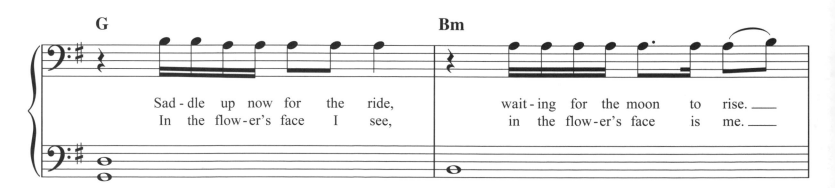

Sad-dle up now for the ride,
In the flow-er's face I see,

wait-ing for the moon to rise. ___
in the flow-er's face is me. ___

Don't want life to pass me by,
I'm gon' watch me grow up now,

don't want life to pass me by. ___
I'm gon' watch me grow up now. ___

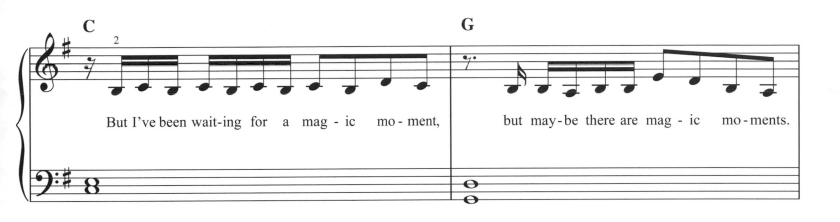

But I've been wait-ing for a mag-ic mo-ment,

but may-be there are mag-ic mo-ments.

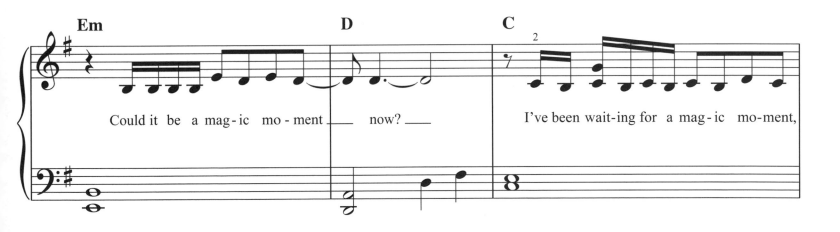

Could it be a mag-ic mo-ment ___ now? ___

I've been wait-ing for a mag-ic mo-ment,

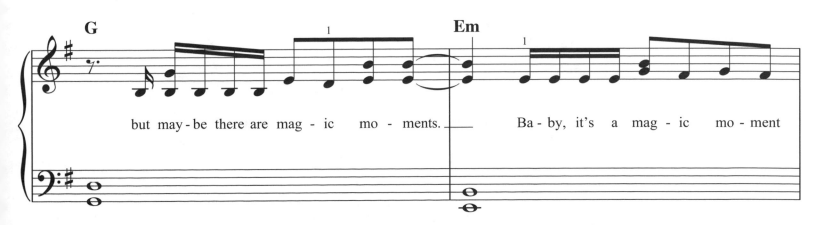

but may-be there are mag-ic mo-ments. ___

Ba-by, it's a mag-ic mo-ment

now. _____ Dar - ling, it's a mag - i - cal, mag - i - cal life, life,

life. ____ Oh, hon - ey, it's a mag - i - cal, mag - i - cal life, life,

life. ____ And, ba - by, it's a mag - i - cal, mag - i - cal life, life,

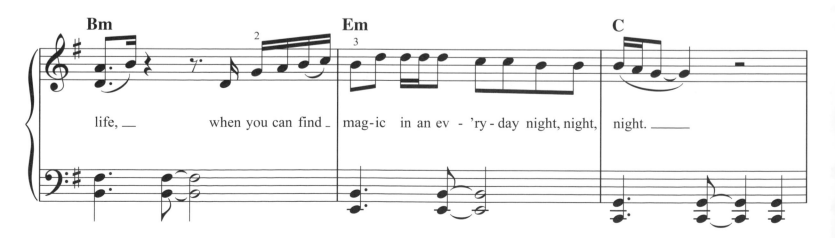

life, __ when you can find __ mag - ic in an ev - 'ry - day night, night, night. _____

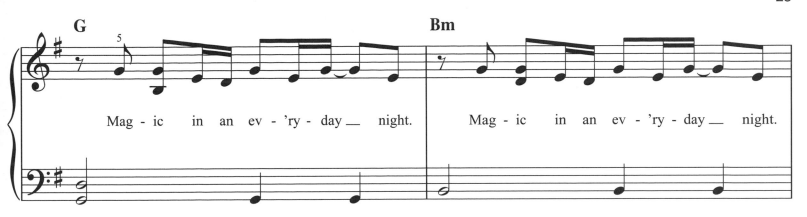

Mag - ic in an ev - 'ry - day — night.   Mag - ic in an ev - 'ry - day — night.

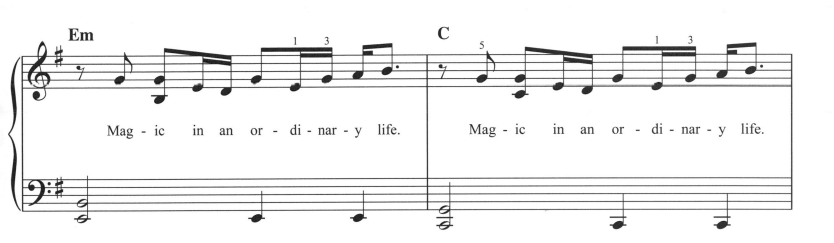

Mag - ic in an or - di - nar - y life.   Mag - ic in an or - di - nar - y life.

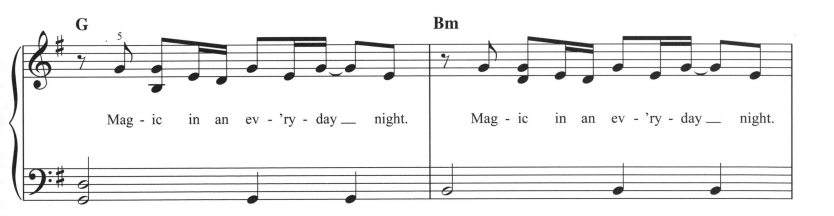

Mag - ic in an ev - 'ry - day — night.   Mag - ic in an ev - 'ry - day — night.

Mag - ic in an or - di - nar - y life.   Mag-ic in an or - di - nar - y life.   Mag-ic in an or - di - nar - y life.

LET ME LIVE

Words and Music by DENISIA ANDREWS,
BRITTANY CONEY, ALI PAYAMI
and KEHLANI PARRISH

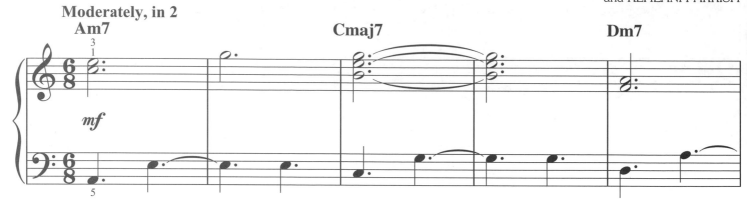

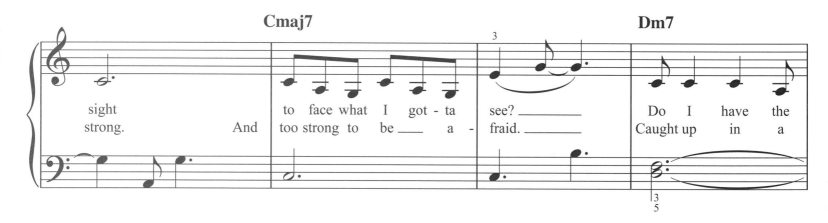

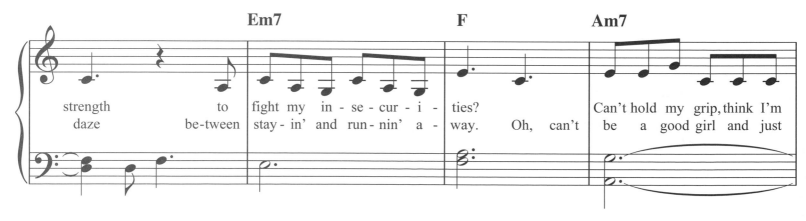

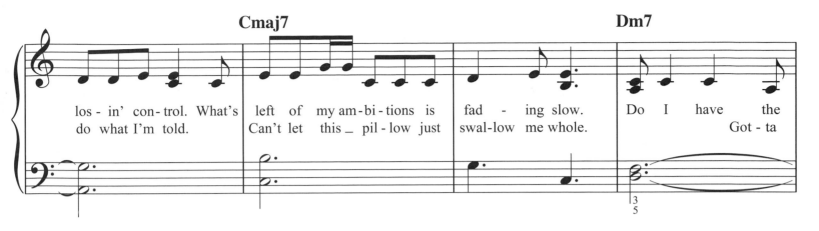

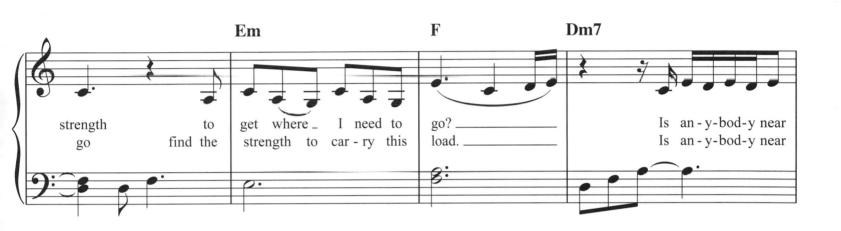

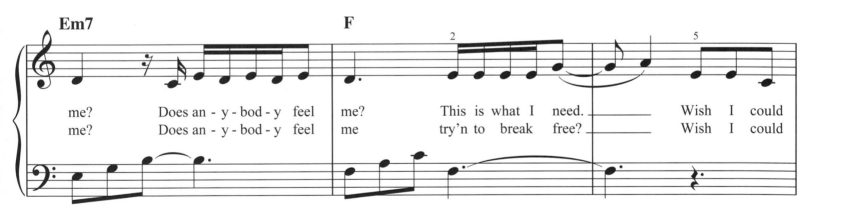

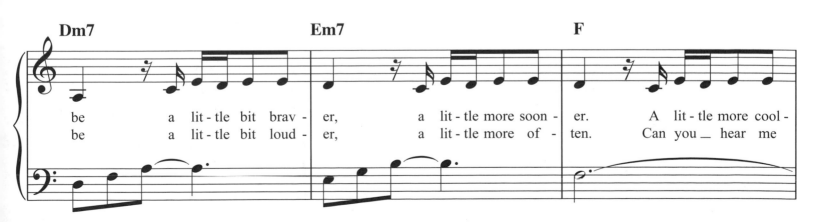

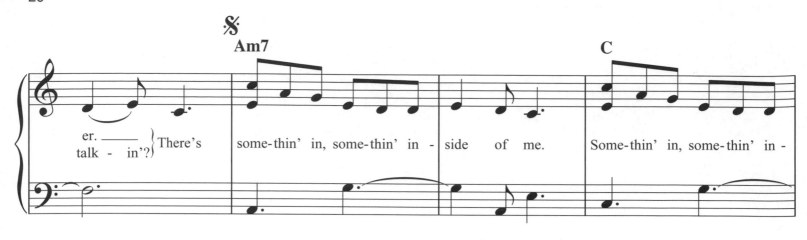

er. _____ talk - in'?) There's some-thin' in, some-thin' in - side of me. Some-thin' in, some-thin' in -

side of me scream-in' oh, _____ let me live out loud. _ Oh, _____ let me

live, let me live. A - Some-thin' in, some-thin' in - side of me.

Some-thin' in, some-thin' in - side of me scream-in' oh, _____ let me

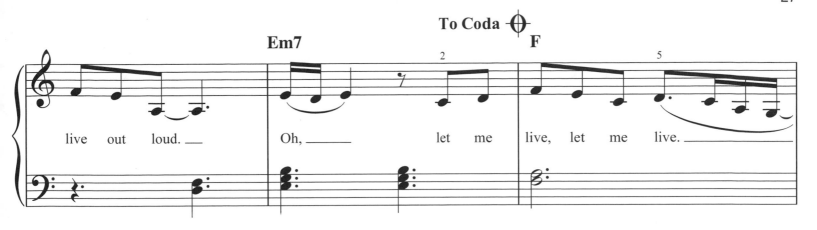

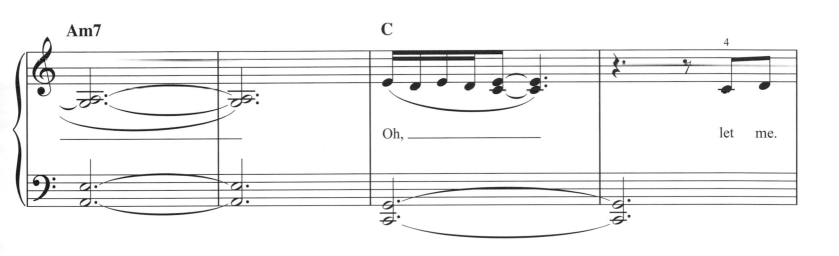

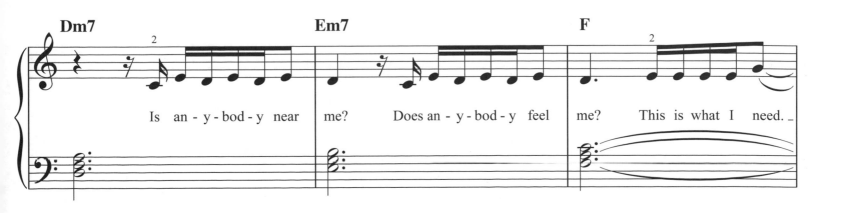

Dm   **Em7**

Wish I could be a lit - tle bit brav - er, a lit - tle more soon -

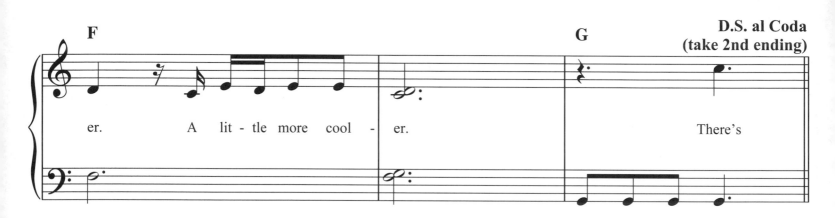

F   **G**   **D.S. al Coda**
(take 2nd ending)

er. A lit - tle more cool - er. There's

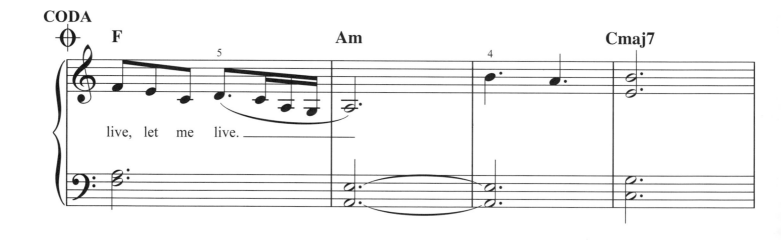

CODA   **F**   **Am**   **Cmaj7**

live, let me live. _____

Dm7   **Em**   **C**

HOME

Music by RAMIN DJAWADI

Very slowly, with freedom

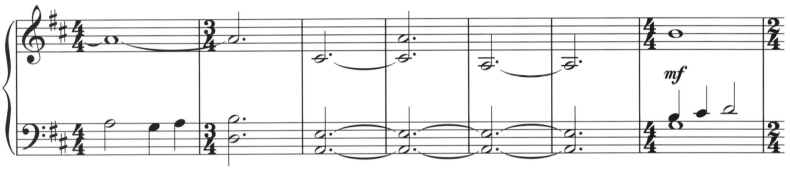

WARRIOR

Music and Lyrics by CHLOE BAILEY
and HALLE BAILEY

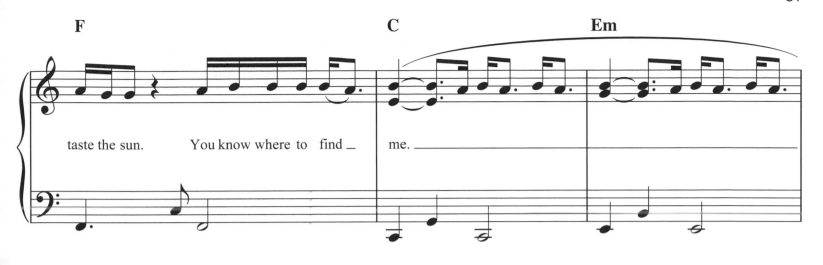

taste the sun. You know where to find __ me. _____

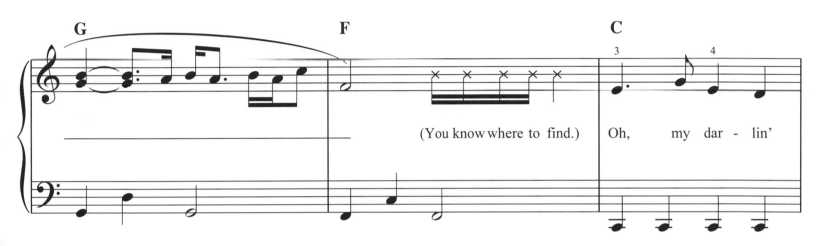

_____ (You know where to find.) Oh, my dar - lin'

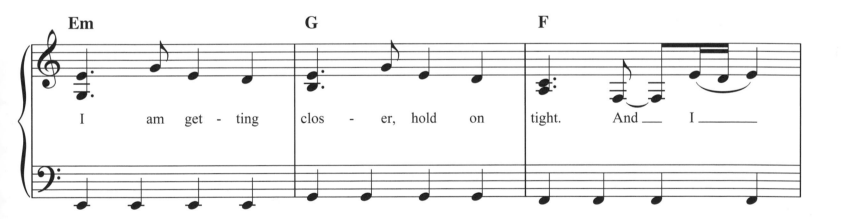

I am get - ting clos - er, hold on tight. And __ I _____

know it has - n't been so eas - y fight - ing for my

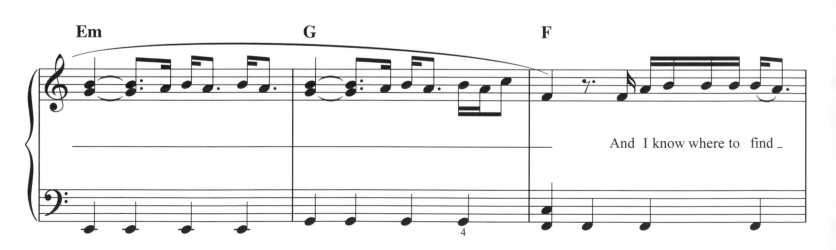

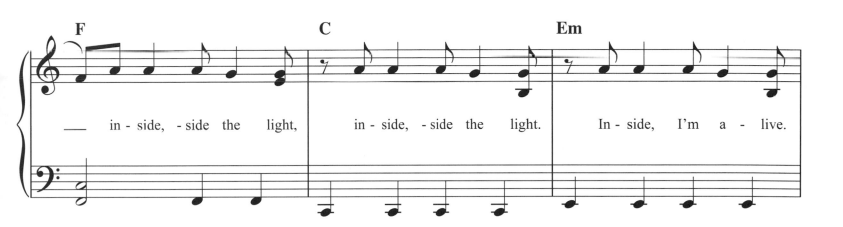

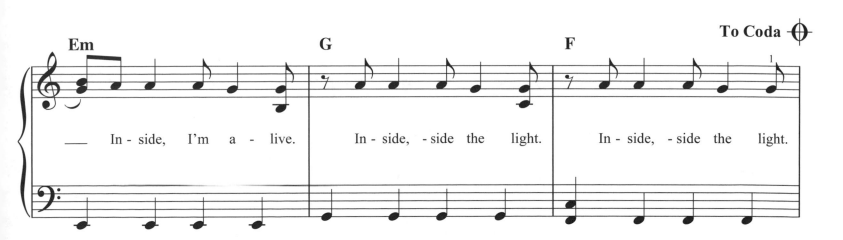

34

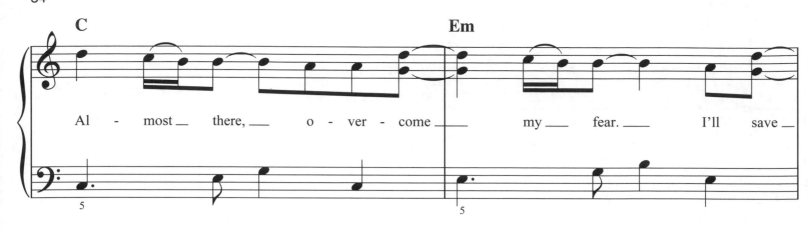

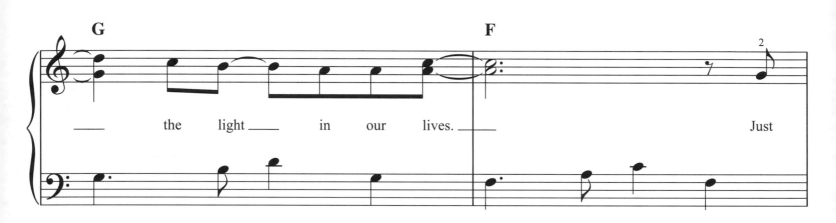

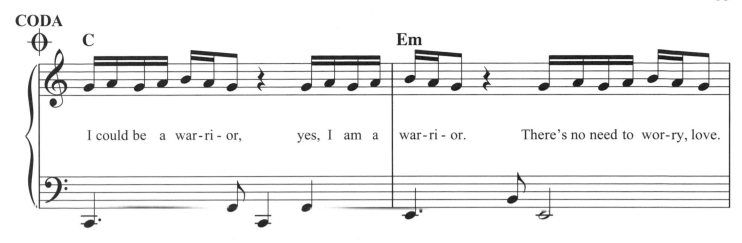

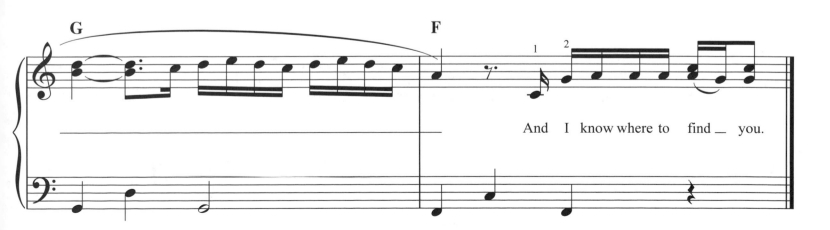

A WRINKLE IN TIME

Music by RAMIN DJAWADI

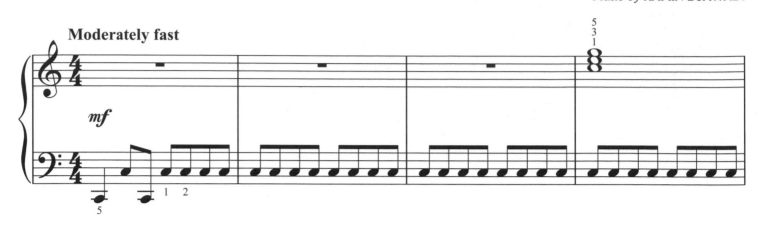

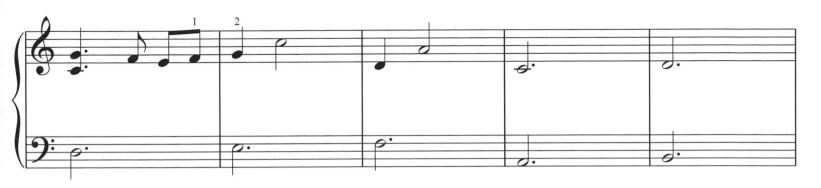

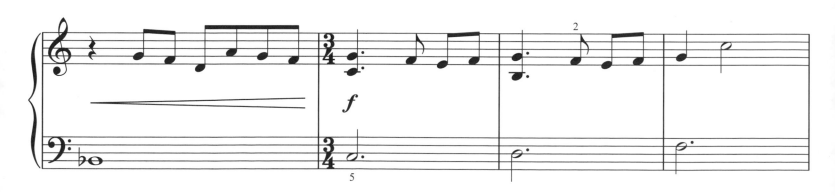

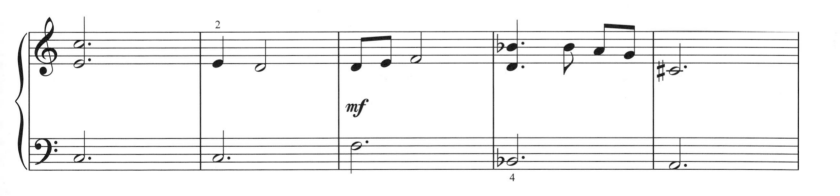

MRS. WHATSIT, MRS. WHO AND MRS. WHICH

Music by RAMIN DJAWADI

Moderately fast

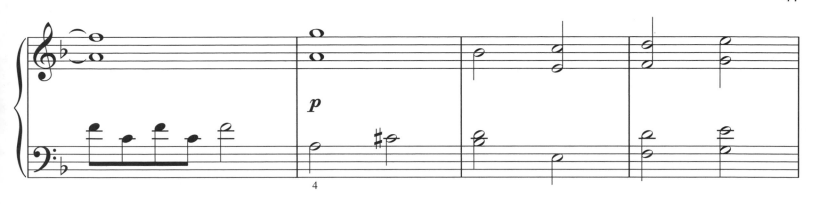

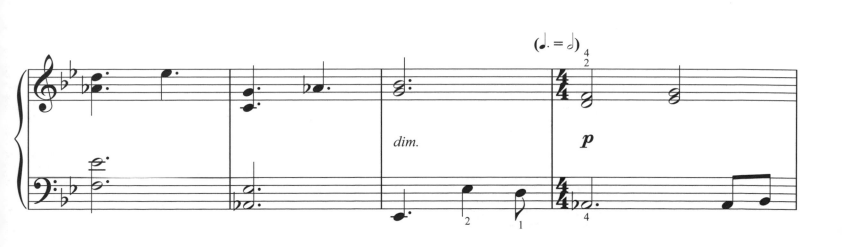

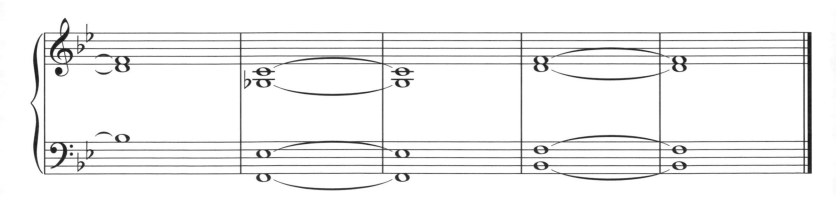

TESSERACT

Music by RAMIN DJAWADI

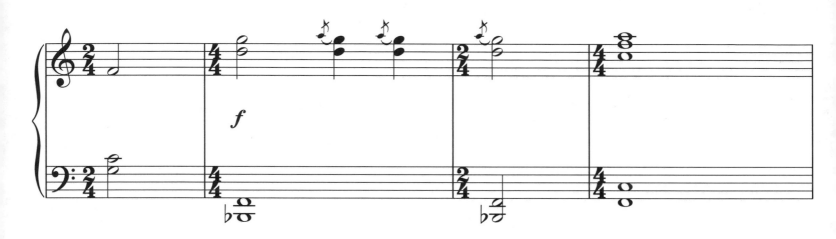

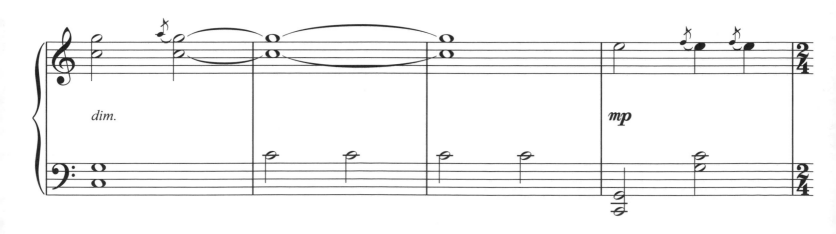

SORRY I'M LATE

Music by RAMIN DJAWADI

Slowly, with freedom

In time

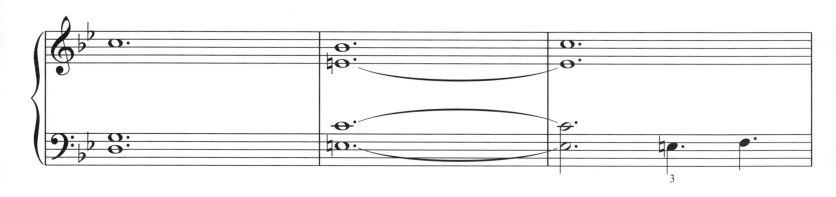

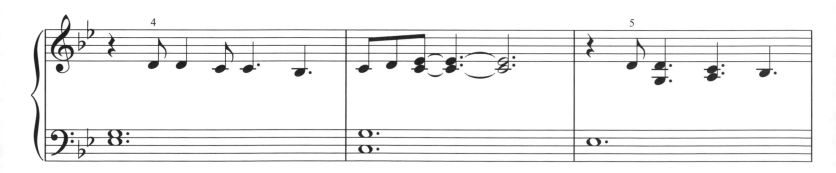

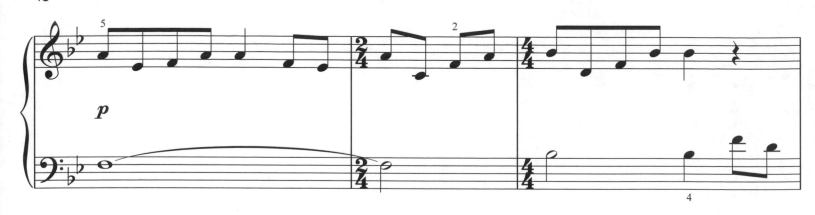

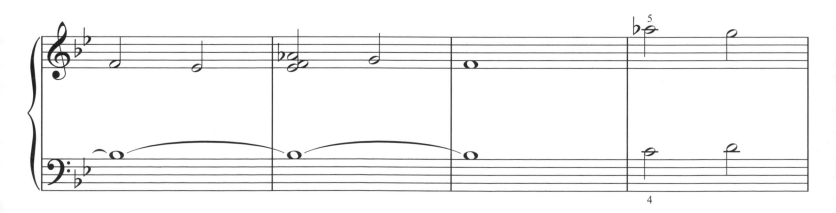

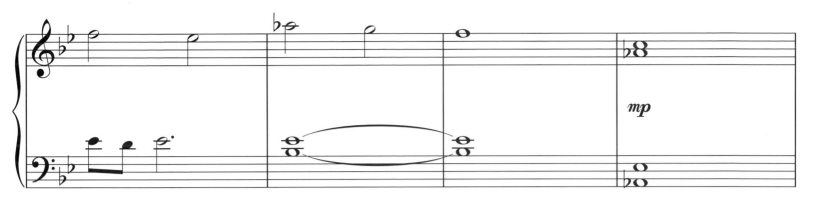

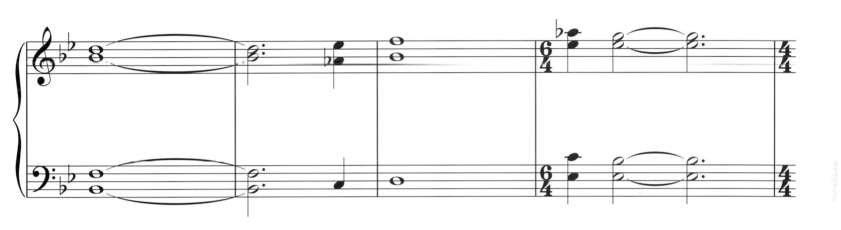

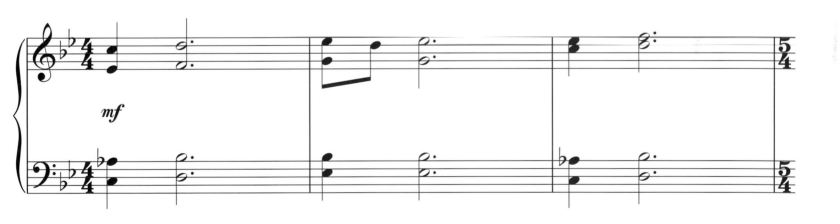

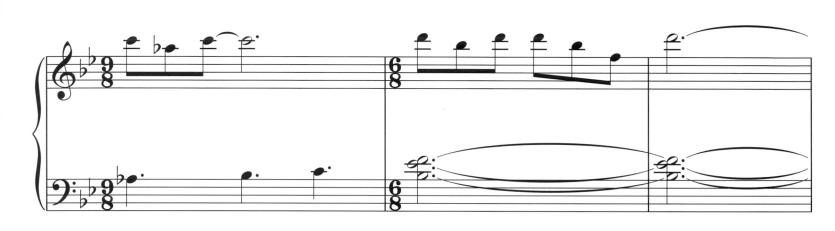

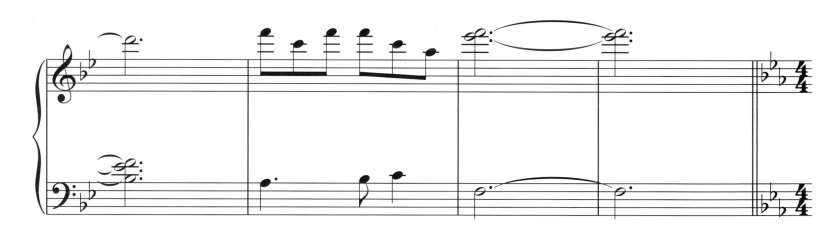

Twice as fast

THE UNIVERSE IS WITHIN ALL OF US

Music by RAMIN DJAWADI

Moderately

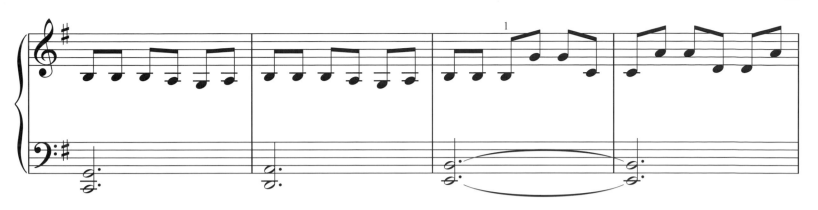